Interview Questions on C Programming

Aditya Chatterjee

Benjamin QoChuk, PhD

© iq.OpenGenus.org

This book is dedicated towards your C programming expertise.

Some of our other books that you must read

Introduction

```
int* x, y;
```

In the above code statement, what is the data type of variable "y"?

97% of programmers would say it is "int *" or "Integer pointer" but the **correct answer is "int"** or "Integer" data type.

In this book, we have presented some of the most interesting questions asked in Interviews for C Programming.

While you answer the question, keep track of your score to see where you stand:

SCORE	LEVEL	NOTE
20 to 25	Excellent	You have a strong hold in C concepts
14 to 19	Good	You are on the right path towards expertise

8 to 13	Nice	You have a strong base in C basics
<= 7	Okay 😐	On your way to master the basics

Each section starts with a question, followed by detailed thoughts on the question to help you think independently and then, we present the answer with the detailed explanation.

You not only answer the question but also get the knowledge of all surrounding ideas. This will prepare you for your upcoming Interview.

Get ready to answer questions

Question 1:

Which of the two statements is faster?

- 0==1
- 0==2

Both are equal	Runtime variation
0==1	0==2

Options:

- Both are equal
- Runtime variation
- 0==1
- 0==2

Thoughts on the question:

In this question, we are dealing with 3 distinct numbers:

- 0
- 1
- 2

As computer represent numbers in binary (base 2) format internally and operate on them, let us represent our number accordingly to get an idea of what we are dealing with:

- 0 = 0000 0000
- 1 = 0000 0001
- 2 = 0000 0010

If we had to implement this problem as an algorithm, we have to potential approaches:

- Serial approach
- Parallel approach

In Serial approach, we would compare the bits in the binary representation one by one till the point we encounter a mismatch. In the worst case, the maximum number of comparisons will be same as the number of bits in the numbers (32 or 64 bits are the most common).

The pseudocode will be as follows:

```
N1, N2 (binary representation)
bits = 64

for i from 0 to bits
    b1 = get i-th bit of N1
    b2 = get i-th bit of N2
    if b1 != b2
        return false // mis-match
return true // match
```

The parallel approach will be similar and the only difference is that the loop iterations are computed all at once as they are independent of each other.

In this case, we compare all bits in unit time as each comparison is done by a different CPU core of the system and usually, systems have several cores (64 cores is common).

The pseudocode looks similar and you can use OpenMP to parallelize the loop:

```
N1, N2 (binary representation)
bits = 64
match = 1

#Parallel execution of the following loop
For i from 0 to bits
    b1 = get i-th bit of N1
    b2 = get i-th bit of N2
    if b1 != b2
        match = 0// mis-match

return match // 1 -> match, 0 -> mis-match
```

With this, the time and space complexity of the program remains the same but the real time performance has improved significantly as the computation at place all at once.

Language point of view

Now, the comparison == is done by C internally so you may be driven by the thought that it depends on the internal implementation followed by C.

This is universally true, but we need to understand that C is one of the earliest and most used Programming languages.

Make your choice now

Answer:

The answer is "**Both comparisons are equal**".

Explanation:

We need to understand that programming languages convert the code to binary code and in that case, simple comparisons (like arithmetic operations) are supported by the system by default.

The closest visualization is the parallel version, but it is not exactly correct. Systems compare two numbers bit by bit at the same time.

As numbers are of fixed number of bits, while comparing internally, we compare blocks of bits as handling a single bit is difficult/ computationally expensive.

Bit is the smallest unit of memory, but Byte is the smallest usable unit of memory.

Question 2:

Inline keyword is used to define a function whose contents will be placed at the point; the function is called. It has another use. What is it?

Remove dependencies	Change linkage behaviour
Optimize code performance	Make code portable

Options:

- Remove dependencies
- Change linkage behavior
- Optimize code performance
- Make code portable

Thoughts on the question:

Inline is used to define a function which will place the entire function code at places where the function has been called at the compilation step. Hence, the size of code increases after the compilation.

Now, you might think that the main objective of a function is to capture common code sections and inline reverses it. The idea is that by using inline we are avoiding the cost of function call (involves system stack) during execution. This results in performance boost.

A common function like multiplying two integers is as follows:

```
static int multiply(int a, int b)
```

Inline is used with the multiply function as follows:

```
static inline int multiply(int a, int b)
```

This is the most common use case of inline keyword:

```c
#include <stdio.h>
// Inline function in C
static inline int multiply(int a, int b)
{
```

```
    return a * b;
}

// Driver code
int main()
{
    int mul = 0, a = 2, b = 5;
    // inline function call
    mul = multiply(a, b);
    printf("Output is: %d\n", mul);
    return 0;
}
```

In this use case, it is a hint to the compiler to optimize the code by placing the function code into the sections where function is called. In other words:

Optimize time over size

Make your choice now.

Answer:

The answer is "**Change linkage behavior**".

Explanation:

Following are the detailed impact of using inline keyword with a function:

- inline void f(void): inline definition is only valid in the current translation unit.
- static inline void f(void): As it is declared as static, the identifier has **internal linkage** and the inline function definition is not available in other translation units.
- extern inline void f(void): As it is declared as extern, the identifier has **external linkage** and the inline function definition is available in external code as well.

Hence, if you notice carefully, we are changing the linkage behavior of functions by using inline keyword along with extern, static or default.

Question 3:

In the following code snippet, what is "x"?

```
char (*x) (char*);
```

pointer to function	character pointer
pointer to char pointer	pointer to char

Options:

- Pointer to function
- Character pointer
- Pointer to char pointer
- Pointer to char

Thoughts on the question:

In C, variables can signify a wide range of things and this makes C a strong programming language. This range of flexibility/ control is not available in other languages like Java.

A variable in C is defined as:

```
char a;
```

In this case, "a" is a variable with data type "character".

A pointer variable is a variable that holds an address to another memory location. You can visualize this as a variable pointing to another variable.

This is important as in C, only "pass by value" is supported where a copy of the variable is pass along different program components.

This makes changing the same variable difficult unless to pass the address value which is done by pointer variables.

It is defined as follows:

```
char* a;
```

In this case, "a" is a variable of type "char*" that is a pointer to a character. We can view "*a" as a variable of type "character" as well.

So, in this case

```
char* a;    IS SAME AS    char (*a);
```

To simplify, our code snippet can be visualized as:

```
char (*x) ();
```

Make your choice now

Answer:

Answer is: **"Pointer to function"**.

x is a pointer to a function that takes char* as a function parameter and returns char.

Let us analyze our code snippet:

```
char (*x) (char*);
```

- By "*x", we know that x is a pointer.
- By () following x, we know it is a function.
- By (char *), we know that the function is taking char* as an input parameter
- By char before x, we know that the return type is char.

Hence, x is a function pointer. In C, variables can point to functions/ code segments as well.

Question 4:

In the following code snippet, what is "y"?

```
char* x, y;
```

compilation error	char variable
pointer to x	char pointer

Options:

- Compilation error
- Char variable
- Pointer to x
- Char pointer

Thoughts on this question

There are three distinct notations of using pointers:

---

1. char* x; (space between x and *)
2. char * x; (space between x, * and char)
3. char *x; (space between char and *)

In terms of functionality, all three notations are same.

The symbol * is used mainly for 3 use cases:

- pointer
- dereference
- multiplication

The position of * in the first notation (int* a) is mainly used as a pointer type.

The position of * in the third notation (int *a) mainly refers to dereference.

Make your choice now

Answer:

| ✘ compilation error | ✔ char variable |
| ✘ pointer to x | ✘ char pointer |

Answer is "**char variable**".

Y is a char variable.

According to C and C++, "*" is associated with the variable and not the data type. Hence, the "*" is linked with X only and not with Y.

To define Y as a pointer like X, the code snippet should be like:

```
char *x, *y;
```

Due to this, the third notation is, usually preferred to avoid this issue.

In general, the first notation is the first choice as:

- One pointer variable should be declared at a time as the memory needs to be allocated as well.
- The third notation (int *a) can be confused with dereference and start using *a as a variable.
- The second notation denotes multiplication and hence, should be avoided.

So, the preferred way to write the above code is as follows:

```
char* x = NULL;
char* y = NULL;
```

Hence, the conclusion is to follow implementation standards to avoid confusion and keep code clean and simple for everyone.

Question 5:

C and C++ are, often, considered to be similar. What is the major difference between the two programming languages?

C++ has more optimizations	C++ is faster
C++ has garbage collection	C++ is OOP, C is not

Options:

- C++ has more optimizations
- C++ is faster
- C++ has garbage collection
- C++ is OOP, C is not

C and C++ both are widely used Programming Languages today and is very similar. In short, most C code can be compiled as C++ code.

There is one significant difference which lead to the creation of C++ as an increment to C.

The C Programming Language was developed in 1972.

The C++ Programming Language was developed in 1979 (Several improvements were added later).

Make your choice now

Answer:

✖ C++ has more optimizations	✖ C++ is faster
✖ C++ has garbage collection	✔ C++ is OOP, C is not

The answer is "**C++ is OOP, C is not**".

The major difference is that C++ is an **Object Oriented Programming language** (OOP) while C is a **general-purpose imperative programming language**.

Due to this, it is difficult to design software systems based on object design in C. There are alternatives in C like struct and union which makes the design of class like design possible to some extent.

For example:

A Binary tree struct in C:

```
typedef struct node{
    struct node * left, * right;
    int value;
} node;
```

A Binary tree class in C++:

```
class BTNode
{
    public:
        int Key;
        BTNode * Left;
        BTNode * Right;
```

```
};
```

You will understand the difference between the two approaches when you extend the structures and build complex operations.

For example, in C++, it is possible to reuse the code for B Tree to create binary tree (using **Inheritance**) but it is not directly possible in C as it does not support Object Oriented Programming.

Question 6:

C is not OOP but struct and union allows one to design class like design. What is the major difference between struct and union features in C?

Union is more space efficient	Struct supports pointer
Union saves all its variables in same location	Struct supports different data types

Options:

- Union is more space efficient
- Struct supports pointer
- Union saves all its variables in same location
- Struct supports different data types

Thoughts on the question:

Struct and union, in simple terms, are ways to group together variables of different data types.

Example of struct:

```
struct Data{
    int a;
    float b;
};
```

The above structure can be used as follows:

```
struct Data data;
data.a = 1;
data.b = 2;
```

Example of union:

```
union Data {
    int a;
    float b;
};
```

The above union can be used as follows:

```
union Data data;
data.a = 1;
data.b = 2;
```

On viewing these example, union and structure looks same but it has a distinct difference due to which these cannot be used interchangeably.

Make your choice now

Answer:

| ✖ Union is more space efficient | ✖ Struct supports pointer |
| ✔ Union saves all its variables in same location | ✖ Struct supports different data types |

The answer is "**Union saves all its variables in same location**".

The major difference is that in struct, all variables are stored in a block of memory that is identified by a name while in union, all variables are stored in the same memory location.

So, union has only one valid value at a time and is useful to represent a variable that can have different datatype at different points. On the other hand, struct is more close to the idea of a standard class.

Hence, if we print the values of the two member values (a and b) for both struct and union, we will get the following values:

- For struct:

a = 1

b = 2

- For union:

a = 93420920 (corrupted)

b = 2

In union, value of a is corrupted as the value of b was set at last which overwrote the value of a.

Question 7:

What is the difference between **#include"..."** and **#include<...>**?

#include \<...> searches in current directory and #include"..." searches in standard fixed directories

#include"..." is memory efficient

#include"..." searches in current directory and #include \<...> searches in standard fixed directories

Both are same

Options:

- #include<> searches in current directory and #include"" searches in standard fixed directories
- #include"" is memory efficient
- #include"" search in current directory and #include<> searches in standard fixed directories
- Both are same

Thoughts on the question:

In C, code can be placed in a separate file which can be loaded as a library for use in multiple client code. These libraries mainly consist of a header file (.h file) which has all function definitions and other macro definitions.

The actual library code resides in a C file or a shared object file which can be linked with the client code during compilation.

In C, there are two ways to include a header file:

- #include <...>
- #include "..."

First format of include:

```
#include <stdio.h>
```

Second format of include:

```
#include "opengenus.h"
```

In general, the first format using <> is used for loading standard libraries while the second format using "" is used for local libraries.

Make your choice now

Answer:

✘ #include \<...> searches in current directory and #include"..." searches in standard fixed directories	✘ #include"..." is memory efficient
✔ #include"..." searches in current directory and #include \<...> searches in standard fixed directories	✘ Both are same

Answer is:

"#include"..." searches in current directory and #include <...> searches in standard fixed directories."

#include"..." searches in current directory and #include<...> searches in standard fixed directories. The include statement with quotes is used to import local libraries which may not be available in standard directories like /lib.

During compilation, we can pass location of directory using -I flag and the compiler will add the mentioned location to the set of predefined locations for #include<..> format.

Hence, #include<...> searches in:

- System directories
- Directories mentioned using -I flag

#include"..." searches in:

- Current directory as of the source code file
- Directories specified by -iqoute flag
- Directories as in the case of #include <...>

Hence, #include"..." can be used in place of #include<...> in most cases but the vice versa may not be simple.

Question 8:

If we pass an array to a function, the value can be changed. What are functions by default in C?

Depends on variable	Pass by reference
Pass by value	Depends on function scope

Options:

- Depends on variable
- Pass by reference
- Pass by value
- Depends on function scope

Thoughts on the question:

In Programming languages, functions are of two types when it comes to function parameters:

- Pass by value
- Pass by reference

In pass by value, a copy of the parameters are passed to the function so if the function modifies the parameters, the copy is modified and the original values remain the same.

In pass by reference, the original variables are passed as parameters so if the function modifies the parameters, the original values are changed.

Hence, consider this example where we are passing an array to a function:

```c
#include <stdio.h>

void set_to_1(int *data);

void set_to_1(int *data) {
    data[0] = 1;
}

int main()
{
    int data[2] = {0, 0};
    printf("before data[0] = %d\n", data[0]);
```

```
    printf("before data[1] = %d\n", data[1]);
    set_to_1(data);
    printf("after data[0] = %d\n", data[0]);
    printf("after data[1] = %d\n", data[1]);
}
```

The output will be as:

```
before data[0] = 0
before data[1] = 0
after data[0] = 1
after data[1] = 0
```

The original value of the array passed to the function has been modified.

Make your choice now

Answer:

Answer is: "**Pass by value**"

All functions in C are pass by value.

The reason why array is modified is because array is represented as a pointer (memory location) where the first element of the array resides.

Hence, when we are passing an array, we are passing a pointer internally.

Pointer variables can be changed as the memory address is passed by value and following the address, the value can be changed. So, the memory address as pointed by the pointer does not change as defined by pass by value.

Question 9:

Extern keyword is used to declare a variable without defining it that is no memory is allocated. Where extern keyword is used?

In static functions	For global variables
In library files	In functions

Options:

- In static functions
- For global variables
- In library files
- In functions

Thoughts on the question:

Extern is used as follows:

```
extern int a;
```

There are two key ideas:

- Declaring a variable
- Defining a variable

Declaring a variable means informing the compiler that a variable exists but no memory has been allocated to it.

Defining a variable means allocating memory to the variable and the compiler acknowledges the existence of the variable.

We can declare a variable multiple time but we can define a variable only once.

By default, when we define a variable as:

```
int a;
```

The memory is allocated statically. If we used malloc and other similar function to allocate memory, the memory is dynamically allocated.

To stop the automatic allocation of memory, we need to use extern.

Make your choice now

Answer:

Extern keyword is used to declare a variable without defining it that is no memory is allocated. It is used to declare variables in library files and in a client code where multiple libraries are imported, there should not be any conflict due to variables.

A variable can be declared multiple times but can be defined only once. Declaring means to specify the variable name and datatype. Defining means to allocate memory.

Question 10:

In International Obfuscated C Code Contest, there was an entry that had the following code snippet. What can you say about J?

```
#define o(X) r(copysign(1, X), exp2(J),
exp2(J))
```

J is a C constant	exp2(J) is a constant value
J depends on value of copysign(1, X)	J must have been defined

Options:

- J is a constant
- Exp2(J) is a constant value
- J depends on value of copysign(1, X)
- J must have been defined

Thoughts on the question:

It is important to understand every code statement and get an idea of all components even if it uses functions/ features you are not aware of.

By using #define, we know we are defining a macro o(X).

Make your choice now

Answer:

✗ J is a C constant	✗ exp2(J) is a constant value
✗ J depends on value of copysign(1, X)	✔ J must have been defined

---

Answer is: "**J must have been defined**"

J must have been defined before this statement. It can be a value or an expression that when computed results in a value.

Question 11:

In the same code snippet, what is meant by copysign?

```
#define o(X) r(copysign(1, X), exp2(J),
exp2(J))
```

Compares sign of the two values

Transfer sign of first value to second value

Finds the difference between the two values

Transfer sign of second value to first value

Options:

- Compares sign of the two values
- Transfer sign of first value to second value
- Finds the difference between the two values
- Transfer sign of second value to first value

Thoughts on the question:

As evident by the options, copysign is a function and it is from a standard C library.

Most functions are descriptive in their name itself. Copysign means the sign is copied.

From the code snippet, we see that copysign takes two values as input and it has to return a single value or make modify the input values as well.

Having a knowledge of various functions across standard C libraries enables one to write highly optimized code. This is because the compilers are optimized for the standard libraries and hence, similar functions defined by a programmer may not be equally optimized.

Make your choice

Answer:

| ✖ Compares sign of the two values | ✖ Transfer sign of first value to second value |
| ✖ Finds the difference between the two values | ✔ Transfer sign of second value to first value |

Answer is: "**Transfer sign of second value to first value**".

copysign is used to modify the sign of the first value based on the second value. If the second value is positive, the first value is made positive and if the second value is negative, the first value is made negative.

Copysign is defined in cmath or math.h library of C.

Question 12:

In the following code snippet, what is "x"?

```
custom_object& x = {1, "iq.opengenus.org"};
```

pointer to user-defined object

reference to user-defined object

user-defined object

memory pointer

Options:

- Pointer to user defined object
- Reference to user defined object
- User defined object
- Memory pointer

Thoughts on the questions:

The data type is **custom_object**. Hence, we know it is a user-defined object which two parameters being passed during initialization:

- 1
- "iq.opengenus.org"

You need to understand what & refers to when used along with an used defined object.

Make your choice now

Answer:

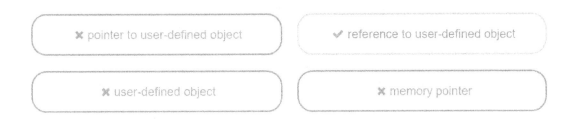

✖ pointer to user-defined object

✔ reference to user-defined object

✖ user-defined object

✖ memory pointer

Answer is "**reference to user-defined object**".

"&" is used after the data type to define references. References to variables are used to pass values in function without making a copy of the original data. This is efficient.

Question 13:

In the following compilation step, what will be the name of the output file?

```
gcc -std=c++14 -c -Iinc/ code.cpp -Llib/
```

a.out	code.o
code.so	code

Options:

- a.out
- code.o
- code.so
- code

Thoughts on the question:

This is an interesting question as it brings the idea that we have control over the compilation process.

Most optimizations in languages like C and C++ resides in the compiler so you will find several compilers which optimizes code for different target systems like CPUs, FPGAs and others.

There are different level of optimizations which is controlled by -O flag.

- -O0 : is the unoptimized level
- -O1 : is the first level of optimizations and it continues till -O3
- -O3 : is the most optimized compiler stage

When we simply compile a code like:

```
gcc code.cpp
```

Then, the output is an executable named a.out. We can control the name of the executable as well.

As an overview, the C code is first compiled into an object file and then, converted into an executable where the object file is linked with all required libraries.

Make your choice now

Answer:

✖ a.out	✔ code.o
✖ code.so	✖ code

Answer is "**code.o**".

The compiler option "-c" is used to get the object file from the given code file instead of directly generating the executable. Object files have an extension ".o".

Get a quick overview of some of the major options:

- -c : get object file (filename.o)
- -o : name of output file
- -I : adds directories where library files are located
- -S : generate assembly code file
- -L : adds directories for library files for the linker

Question 14:

In C Standard, the operator [] is defined as an arithmetic expression and used in array notation as well. What is the meaning of a[b]?

*a + b

*(a+b)

a + *(b)

a + b

Options:

- *a+b
- *(a+b)
- a+*(b)
- a+b

The C Standard mentions that [] is an arithmetic operator just like +, -, / and *.

Moreover, an array is defined by two values:

- Memory address of the first element
- Length of array

Make your choice now

Answer:

✘ *a + b	✔ *(a+b)
✘ a + *(b)	✘ a + b

Answer: ***(a + b)**

a[b] is the bth index in array a. So, the memory address of this element is denoted by *(a+b).

---

a is not an array but a memory address. a + b is the memory address with b steps from a that is the bth element of the array.

Note that by b steps, we mean b * c steps where c is the unit step. c is the size of the data type of the array. So, if the unit size of 4 bytes, then the 5th element will be starting after 16 bytes from the beginning.

*(a + b) means the value that is stored at the memory location (a + b).

Hence, a[b] = b[a] where b is an integer.

Question 15:

In the following code snippet, what is "x"?

```
int ** const x;
```

const pointer to pointer to int	pointer
const pointer to const int	pointer to const int

Options:

- Const pointer to pointer to int
- Pointer
- Const pointer to const int
- Pointer to const int

Thoughts on the questions:

A pointer in C is a variable that points to a memory location which in turn can point to another location or be the starting point of a set of values.

This enables programmers to have greater control and implement a wide range of ideas.

- "int * a" can be seen as an array or a pointer.
- "int ** a" can be seen as a 2D array or a pointer to a pointer.

```
int * x;
int ** x;
```

The challenge is to understand the significant of const in the statement.

Make your choice now

Answer:

✔ const pointer to pointer to int	✖ pointer
✖ const pointer to const int	✖ pointer to const int

Answer: "**const pointer to pointer to int**"

"x" is a const pointer to pointer to int. The expression can be seen as "int * (* const) x;"

Const pointer means the pointer cannot be modified. Hence, the first dimension of the array will point to the same location as initially initialized.

Note that this does not mean that the values are constant/ cannot be changed.

These statements will make the idea clear:

- **int * a** : pointer to an int

```
int * a;
```

We can modify both the pointer and the value it points to.

- **int * const a** : const pointer to an int

```
int * const a;
```

We cannot modify the pointer as it is constant. The value it points to can be changed.

- **const int * a** : pointer to const int

```
const int * a;
```

We can modify the pointer but we cannot modify the value (int) it points to as it is constant.

- **int const * a** : pointer to const int

```
int const * a;
```

We can modify the pointer but we cannot modify the value (int) it points to as it is constant.

- **const int * const a** : const pointer to const int

```
const int * const a;
```

We cannot modify the pointer nor the value it points to.

With this, you should have a good foundation in pointers.

Question 16:

Which of the following error code is returned by C code when "No such file or directory" error is encountered?

ENOTFOUND	ENOENT
ENOFILE	EINVAL

Options:

- ENOTFOUND
- ENOENT
- ENOFILE
- EINVAL

Thoughts on the question:

Error codes in C are macros that point to Integer values defining the error type. It is defined in the header file errno.h.

The header file can be included as:

```
#include <errno.h>
```

When a function is called, a global variable errno is set to a numerical value which corresponds to an error if encountered.

One common error is "File not found" which is the question. The numerical error code is 2.

```
#include <stdio.h>
#include <errno.h>

int main()
{
    FILE * fp;
    fp = fopen("no_file.txt", "r");
```

```
    printf("errno: %d\n ", errno);
    return 1;
}
```

In this code, the variable errno is set to 2 if the file being opened by fopen does not exist.

All standard error has a numeric value and a corresponding MACRO.

Make your choice now

Answer:

✗ ENOTFOUND	✔ ENOENT
✗ ENOFILE	✗ EINVAL

Answer: "**ENOENT**"

ENOENT stands for "Error NO ENtry" or "Error NO ENtity" and is used to denote the "No such file or directory" error.

Hence, in the header file errno.h, the macro ENOENT is 2.

Question 17:

size_t is an unsigned data type returned by the common function sizeof(). In which header file, size_t is defined?

stddef.h	stdlib.h
math.h	string.h

Options:

- Stddef.h
- Stdlib.h
- Math.h
- String.h

Standard header files in C are important as it enables one to bring the full potential of a C implementation. Every header has a different use and can become confusing at times.

A quick overview of the purpose of different header files are:

- stdio.h : For input and output functions
- math.h : For math related functions
- string.h : For string related operations
- stdlib.h : Defines variable types and serves as a library for basic utilities
- stddef.h : For standard C definitions/ macros
- errno.h : For definition of standard errors

A header file is included as:

```
#include <math.h>
```

Make your choice now

Answer:

| ✔ stddef.h | ✘ stdlib.h |
| ✘ math.h | ✘ string.h |

The answer is "**stddef.h**".

size_t is defined in stddef.h but it can be imported through stdlib.h as well.

The header file can be included as:

```
#include <stddef.h>
```

Question 18:

To run a system command from C code, what command can be used?

syst()	system()
setenv()	system.run()

Options:

- syst()
- system()
- setenv()
- system.run()

Thoughts on the question:

One thing to understand is that the main code runs on a parent thread and any system command that is executed within C starts a new child thread.

So, when the program exists, the changes done by the code vanishes if it is linked with the current terminal session. This is because as the parent process exits the child process has to exits as well.

One such property is setting environment variables. If we set environment variables using a C code, it will not reflect after the program exits.

Make your choice now

Answer:

Answer: "**system()**"

system is a standard call in C that is used to run system commands directly from the C code. Note that the changes are reflected only in the child of current shell and is not observed as the program execution completes.

To set environment variables like OMP_NUM_THREADS, the command on Linux systems are:

```
export OMP_NUM_THREADS=16
```

The same thing can be achieved in C code using the system() call as:

```
system("export OMP_NUM_THREADS=16");
```

Another alternative is the setenv() function which can be used as follows:

```
setenv("OMP_NUM_THREADS", 16);
```

Question 19:

C did not have a boolean data type. In C99 (release in 1999), it was first supported. What is the new boolean data type named?

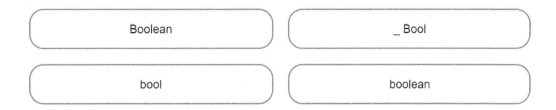

| Boolean | _ Bool |
| bool | boolean |

Options:

- Boolean
- _bool
- Bool
- boolean

Thoughts on the question:

When C was originally designed, the inventors did not add support for a standard Boolean data type. It is understandable as C is a very early language and had very few working references.

Later, C was widely adopted, and programmers noticed this limitation and made their workarounds.

They defined their own Boolean data type and this approach was widely adopted.

Later in 1999, the new C standard (named C99) was released which included the in-built support for a Boolean data type.

One point that was considered is that the new standard should not break existing code. Due to this, the new Boolean data type should not create any conflicts with the work-arounds created by programmers.

Make your choice now

Answer:

✘ Boolean	✔ _ Bool
✘ bool	✘ boolean

Answer is "**_Bool**"

_Bool is the original boolean data type. It was named as such to avoid breaking existing code as many developers developed workarounds with their own version of boolean.

Hence, the bool data type in C requires us to import a header file.

Question 20:

Boolean datatype only needs 0 or 1 value which can be represented by a single bit. What is the memory size of boolean data type in C?

1 bit	2 bit
16 Byte	1 Byte

Options:

- 1 bit
- 2 bit
- 16 Byte
- 1 Byte

Thoughts on the question:

Every data requires a minimum number of bits to be correctly represented. Computer systems all around

---

the World has adopted the binary representation. One must understand that this may not be the most space optimal representation.

The most optimal representation depends on the data that needs to be represented. Algorithms like Huffman encoding are designed to find the optimal representation.

As we cannot change representations randomly, we need a standard and hence, we follow the binary representation.

In this idea, 1 will take less number of bits to represent when compared to 99.

In Programming languages, integers have standard size say 4 bytes. So, the space consumed by 1 is same as 99. 4 bytes will have 32 bits that means it can represent 2^{32} distinct integers.

The case of Boolean data type is unique.

Make your choice now

Answer:

The answer is "**1 Byte**".

Though Boolean data type needs only 1 bit, it has to use 1 byte (that is 8 bits) as in Computing systems, 8 bits or 1 byte is the smallest unit of memory that can be used. Operations can be performed on bits but in terms of memory allocation, the lowest level one can access in 1 byte.

So, in every boolean variable, 1 bit is used and the other 7 bits are vacant.

Question 21:

What is the difference between calloc and malloc in C (for memory allocation)?

calloc for contiguous allocation	malloc initializes memory; calloc does not
malloc for contiguous allocation	calloc initializes memory; malloc does not

Options:

- Calloc for contiguous allocation
- Malloc initializes memory; calloc does not
- Malloc for contiguous allocation
- Calloc initializes memory; malloc does not

Thoughts on the question:

C provides a good control over memory allocation in the sense that there are two modes:

- Static memory allocation

- Dynamic memory allocation

The main advantage of Dynamic memory allocation is that we control the amount of memory that is allocated, and we can free the memory once used.

This is important in systems that maintain a common memory and different processes, or components use parts of the memory.

One example is memory pool as maintained by Java or software systems like TensorFlow.

Malloc and Calloc are two significant functions to allocate memory in C.

Malloc is used as follows:

```
data = (data_type*) malloc(units * size);
```

Calloc is used as follows:

```
data = (data_type*) calloc(units, size);
```

Make your choice now

Answer:

✖ calloc for contiguous allocation	✖ malloc initializes memory; calloc does not
✖ malloc for contiguous allocation	✔ calloc initializes memory; malloc does not

Answer is "**Calloc initializes memory; malloc does not**".

The only difference is that calloc initializes the memory it allocates to 0 and is slightly slower than malloc for

---

this extra step. In case of malloc, memory may have garbage value.

Question 22:

"assert" checks value at runtime. How to check values at compile time to avoid runtime failures?

Not possible	Use define macro
Use assert with extern	Use -!!(e)

Options:

- Not possible
- Use define macro
- Use assert with extern
- Use -!!(e)

Thoughts on the question:

Assert is a macro that is defined in the header file assert.h which is frequently used for verifying values.

Assert takes in an expression and return true if the expression evaluates to true or else it returns false.

It is used as follows:

```
assert( data >= 10)
```

This expression evaluates at run time but what if we need to do such check during compile time.

Make your choice now

Answer:

✖ Not possible	✖ Use define macro
✖ Use assert with extern	✔ Use -!!(e)

Answer is: "Use -!!(e)"

Macros like -!!(e) are used to do compile-time checks and are an alternative to assert() which perform run-time checks.

It is used as follows:

```
#define BUILD_BUG_ON_ZERO(e)
        (sizeof(struct { int:-!!(e); }))
```

It is a way to check if expression e evaluates to 0 or not and raise a build error based on the value. In this case, -!!(e) will return 0 if e = 0 or else -1.

Question 23:

Memory leak is the case when the pointer to memory is destroyed but memory is not freed. Dangling pointer is a different memory issue. What is it?

a void pointer (void*)	pointer to freed memory
Undefined pointer	pointer that does not exist

Options:

- A void pointer (void*)
- Pointer to freed memory
- Undefined pointer
- Pointer that does not exist

Thoughts on the question:

C has provided great control over memory but it is, also an overhead compared to other languages as the programmer need to make sure no memory issues should come up.

A common issue is "**segmentation fault**".

It occurs when one tries to access memory which has not been allocated for use.

Memory leak is another significant problem where memory is not freed due to this, memory is allocated continuously and ultimately, the system runs out of usable memory.

Whenever, memory is dynamically allocated like:

```
data = (data_type*) malloc(units * size);
```

then, it is a good practice to free the allocated memory at the end of the program or at the point where the memory is not used further.

```
free(data);
```

Make your choice now

Answer:

✖ a void pointer (void*)	✔ pointer to freed memory
✖ Undefined pointer	✖ pointer that does not exist

Answer is "**pointer to freed memory**"

Dangling pointer refers to the problem where a pointer is used which used to pint to a valid memory location but the memory has been deallocated in between. Due to this, the pointer does point to the same memory but it is not being used in the same way.

There can be another pointer variable that can point to the same memory location and hence, create conflicts in memory data.

Question 24:

What is the issue with wild pointers?

Can point to uninitialized memory	Can point to non-existant memory
Can point to garbage value	Does not point to anything

Options:

- Can point to uninitialized memory
- Can point to non-existent memory
- Can point to garbage value
- Does not point to anything

Thoughts on the question:

Wild pointers are pointers that has been declared but not initialized to a specific value.

In C, when we do not initialize a variable, it may or may not have garbage value. In other Programming languages like Java, this is not the case.

A wild pointer:

```
int* a;        // A wild pointer

int* a = 2; // Not  a wild pointer
```

Make your choice now

Answer:

Answer is "**Can point to non-existent memory**"

As wild pointers are uninitialized pointers, it can point to any value and it can also, point to a memory location that does not exist.

Due to this, program can crash if it is accessed. Hence, it is important to initialize pointers to NULL value.

```
int* a = NULL;
```

Question 25:

Given x is an integer, which expression can be used to check endianness of a System?

Options:

- **x
- (int)(&x)+48
- *x+48
- (char*)(&x)

Thoughts on the question:

Endianness refers to the order in which bytes are stored (from left or right). There are two major types:

- Big endian: Bytes are stored from left to right (least significant digit to the left)
- Little endian: Bytes are stored from right to left (least significant digit to the right)

Consider a data in hexadecimal 0x0A0B0C0D.

In little endian, it is stored as:

0D	0C	0B	0A

In big endian, it is stored as:

0A	0B	0C	0D

In system like networking systems, the order of bytes is important as it determines the how the data is transferred and processed.

Make your choice now

Answer:

Answer is: "(char*)(&x)".

This is because this expression allows us to access each byte separately starting from the left end (to right end) just like an array.

The key ideas are:

- Char is of size 1 byte
- char* can be seen as an array of characters
- &x is the address of the variable x

Hence, the expression returns the address of x and casts it as an array.

The first byte can be accessed as:

```
(char*)(&x)[0]
```

Similarly, the second byte can be accessed as:

```
(char*)(&x)[1]
```

As we should know how the bytes should be stored internally for each case, we can verify it by going through the bytes.

If x is 1, then we need to check only the first byte if it is 1 or 0.

With this, you should have a strong hold of endianness of the system.

What is your score?

If you scored high, congratulations.

If you scored low, no problem. Go through our explanations carefully, put the ideas into practice and attempt the questions again in a few days.

iq.opengenus.org

 team@opengenus.org

 discuss.opengenus.org

 amazon.opengenus.org

 internship.opengenus.org

Share your feedback with us.

Our other popular books:

Keep learning and Stay hydrated.

www.ingramcontent.com/pod-product-compliance
Lightning Source LLC
LaVergne TN
LVHW081531050326
832903LV00025B/1728